EVERY
with Je
FOR GROWING CHRISTIANS

THE ARMOUR
OF GOD

BY SELWYN HUGHES

QUIET TIME

*What awe,
what wonder,
for tiny man on
frail earth
to realise that
size
is no measure of
worth
in God's enormous eyes.*

A CALL TO ARMS

For Reading and Meditation: Ephesians 6:10–13

"For our struggle is not against flesh and blood ..." (v. 12)

We begin today a detailed study of the spiritual protection that is available to every Christian when doing battle with the devil. All those who have committed their lives to Jesus Christ know (or should know) that there are in existence two orders and two kingdoms, the forces of which are locked together in mortal combat. One is the kingdom of God and the other is the kingdom of the devil. And Christians, whether they like it or not, are thrust right on to the cutting edge of that conflict.

TRAINING FOR COMBAT

Many Christians are pacifists when it comes to the matter of earthly warfare, but no one can be a pacifist when it comes to the matter of spiritual warfare. Once we enlist in the army of God, we are then expected to train in the art of offensive and defensive spiritual warfare. At certain times and occasions in the Christian life, we find ourselves in a battle that demands fierce hand-to-hand combat with the forces of darkness, and unless we know how to handle these situations, we shall easily be overthrown.

The Bible shows us that the devil and his minions are bitter enemies of God, but because they are powerless against the Almighty, they turn their concentrated attention on those who are His followers – you and I. Did you notice how many times in the passage before us today the word "against" appears? It occurs six times in all, showing that when a person comes over on to the side of Jesus Christ, he is immediately identified as being for God and against the devil. There can be no compromise on this issue, no peaceful co-existence pact. To be *for* God is to be *against* the devil.

To be for God is to be against the devil.

Gracious and loving Father, help me get my perspectives clear. Train me in the art of spiritual warfare so that I will be able to resist every onslaught of the devil and come through every conflict victoriously. In Jesus' Name. Amen.

IS THERE A PERSONAL DEVIL?

For Reading and Meditation: John 8:36–44

"... He was a murderer from the beginning ..." (v. 44)

Surprising as it may sound, some Christians do not believe in a personal devil. A modern-day theologian writes: "Let us put to sleep this idea of a personal devil who walks about with a pitchfork seeking to tumble people into hell. Evil is not a personality but an influence – it is just the darkness where the light ought to be."

APTLY NAMED

While I agree that the picture of a personal devil walking about with a pitchfork and with horns and a tail is not to be found anywhere in Scripture, the concept of a personal devil is found everywhere in Scripture. One evidence of this is the fact that many of the names given to him denote personality: Satan, deceiver, liar, murderer, accuser, tempter, prince of the power of the air, and so on. Listen to what someone has written on this subject:

> "Men don't believe in the devil now, as their
> fathers used to do,
> They reject one creed because it's old, for
> another because it's new,
> But who dogs the steps of the toiling saint, who
> spreads the net for his feet,
> Who sows the tares in the world's broad fields
> where the Saviour sows His wheat,
> They may say the devil has never lived, they
> may say the devil has gone,
> But simple people would like to know – who
> carries his business on?"

Take it from me, whether or not you believe in the devil, he most certainly believes in you.

Whether or not you believe in the devil, he most certainly believes in you.

Father, help me see that it is to Satan's advantage for me not to believe in him. Then he can do his evil work unresisted. Over these coming weeks, unfold to me the strategies I need to overcome him. In Christ's Name I ask it. Amen.

SATAN – AN EVIL INTELLIGENCE

For Reading and Meditation: Matthew 4:1–11

*"Jesus said to him, 'Away from me, Satan!
For it is written ...'"* (v. 10)

We said yesterday that some of the names given to the devil in Scripture – deceiver, liar, murderer, and so on – show him to be a real personality. But if more proof is required, then consider the passage that is before us today.

CHRIST'S CONFRONTATION

Jesus is seen here in direct confrontation with the devil, even engaging in conversation with him. Some liberal theologians explain this in these terms – Christ (so they say) was having a conversation with the dark thoughts that arose from within His nature, so any "devil" that was present was subjective, not objective.

If we allow that Christ had dark thoughts within His nature, then the whole scheme of redemption tumbles like a pack of cards, for a saviour who is not perfect could never fully atone for our sins. As Dr Handley Moule puts it: "A saviour who is not perfect is like a bridge broken at one end and is not a reliable passage of access." Once we try to get around Scripture, we create endless difficulties for ourselves and finish up looking foolish. Far better to accept the Bible as it stands and believe its testimony on everything.

Actually, as we said yesterday, it is to Satan's advantage to get us to believe that he is not a personal being, for if there is no personal devil, there can be no personal resistance. Don't allow yourself to be deceived into thinking that the term "devil" is a synonym for the evil influence that is in the world. The devil is more than an evil influence; he is an evil intelligence. Only when we recognise this fact will we be motivated to take the steps to effectively resist him.

Recognising the devil is an evil intelligence motivates us to resist him.

Father, help me see that the first step in spiritual warfare is to "know the enemy". For until I know and understand my enemy, I will not be able to defeat him. Deepen my knowledge of these important truths, I pray. In Jesus' Name. Amen.

"Who Cleft the Devil's Foot?"

For Reading and Meditation: Isaiah 14:9–15 & Ezekiel 28:11–19

"You said in your heart ... 'I will make myself like the Most High.'" (Isaiah 14:13–14)

The question is often asked, especially by new Christians: Just who is the devil, and where does he come from? The seventeenth-century poet John Donne wrote that there were two things he could not fathom: "Where all the past years are, and who cleft the devil's foot". The origin, existence and activities of the devil have always been among man's most puzzling problems. The books of Isaiah and Ezekiel give us a very clear picture, however, of what someone has called "The Rise and Fall of the Satanic Empire".

THE FIRST REBELLION

Jesus, while He was here on earth, said one day to His disciples: "I saw Satan falling from heaven as a flash of lightning" (Luke 10:18, TLB). Before he was known as the devil, Satan was called Lucifer and was created as a perfect angelic being. The passages before us today show him to have been a beautiful and morally perfect being. "You were the perfection of wisdom and beauty" (Ezekiel 28:12, TLB). "You were perfect in all you did from the day you were created" (Ezekiel 28:15, TLB).

Upright, beautiful, brilliant and with an enormous capacity for achievement, God entrusted Lucifer with the highest of all the offices in the interstellar universe. "I appointed you to be the anointed guardian cherub. You had access to the holy mountain of God ... O overshadowing cherub" (Ezekiel 28:14 & 16, TLB). In his heart, however, arose a rebellious thought: "I will make myself like the Most High". Five times that phrase "I will" is used in this passage. Those two little words, "I will", reveal what lies behind the awful blight of sin – a created will coming into conflict with the will of the Creator.

Sin results from a created will coming into conflict with the will of the Creator.

O Father, now that I see the real issue that lies behind sin – a created will colliding with the will of the Creator – help me constantly to align my will with Your will. In Jesus' Name I ask it. Amen.

SATAN'S FORCES
For Reading and Meditation: Jude verses 1–13

"... the angels who did not keep their positions of authority ... these he has kept in darkness, bound with everlasting chains ..." (v. 6)

We continue with the question: Just who is the devil and where does he come from? We saw yesterday that the devil was created as a wise and morally perfect being (then known as Lucifer) who aspired to take over the throne of God and thus usurp the position of his Creator. Once that happened, Lucifer was expelled from heaven, together with the other angels who had sensed and shared his rebellious attitude. This is the fall from heaven that Jesus told His disciples He had witnessed.

ASSESSING THE OPPOSITION
Since his fall from heaven, Satan, apparently losing little of his administrative skill, has marshalled these fallen angels (now known as demons) into a hostile force to work against God and His creation. We do not know just how many angels fell with Satan, but doubtless it must have been a colossal number. Once when Jesus asked a demonic, "What is your name?" (Luke 8:30), the demons answered: "Legion." If they were telling the truth, the man was controlled by thousands of demons. A Roman legion contained 6,000 men!

It is little wonder, then, that the apostle Paul warned the Ephesians that they were involved in a tremendous spiritual conflict: "We are not fighting against people made of flesh and blood, but against persons without bodies – the evil rulers of the unseen world, those mighty satanic beings and great evil princes of darkness who rule this world" (Ephesians 6:12, TLB). Is it any wonder our world is in the mess it is in today? One of America's founding fathers said: "If men will not be governed by God, then they will be ruled by tyrants." How sad that men and women actually choose to be governed by Satan rather than by God.

"If men will not be governed by God, then they will be ruled by tyrants."

O God my Father, I am so thankful that I have left the tyranny and rule of Satan to come under the sway of Your eternal and everlasting kingdom. May I come more and more under its sway – hour by hour and day by day. In Jesus' Name I pray. Amen.

"THE SECOND COMING OF SATAN"

For Reading and Meditation: I Timothy 4:1–16

"… in the last times some in the church will turn away from Christ and become eager followers of teachers with devil-inspired ideas." (v. 1, TLB)

If we are to be effective in the art of spiritual warfare, then we must see that mankind's fiercest foe is not death or disease, but the diabolical deceiver we know as the devil. He is behind all our individual woes and international wars. He is the one who instigates all our crime and violence. He writes the script for human sorrow, sickness and death. That is not to say that mankind does not bear some responsibility for the things I mention, but the motivation for these things springs directly from the devil. And there are signs that the devil's mission is hotting up – just as our text for today predicted it would.

SATAN'S PUBLICISTS

I think it is safe to say that in this generation, the devil is getting more exposure than he has had in any previous generation since the beginning of recorded time. Not so many years ago, *The Exorcist* broke all box office records, grossing over 150 million dollars. It was followed by a spate of films on the subject of the paranormal – *The Omen, The Antichrist* and many others – so much so that someone has described this age as the Second Coming of Satan.

In songs, in art, in the theatre, Satan is making his presence felt in a new and powerful way. And now the so-called science of parapsychology has given him admittance to the halls of academia. How sad that some colleges and universities present accredited courses on satanism but bar any reference to the teachings of Jesus Christ. Make no mistake about it, the devil is on the march. But don't let that thought trouble you too deeply, for the Scripture shows it is to be a march to oblivion (Revelation 20:10).

Man's fiercest foe is not death or disease, but the devil.

O God, I am so grateful for the assurances of Scripture. They come to me at the moment I most need them and hold me fast when the strongest currents threaten to sweep me away from my spiritual moorings. Thank You, dear Father. Amen.

DANGER – THE DEVIL AT WORK

For Reading and Meditation: 1 Peter 5:1–11

"… Your enemy the devil prowls around like a roaring lion …" (v. 8)

We said yesterday that the spiritual battle between Satan and God is hotting up. When I made a similar statement in a meeting at which I spoke some time ago, a woman came up to me and said: "I think you are giving too much credit to the devil. He is such an insignificant person compared to God that we ought not even mention his name." In one way I can sympathise with this view, for when you listen to some Christians talk, you get the impression that they have a small God and a big devil.

THE FORGOTTEN ADVERSARY

However, it would be unrealistic to think that we can go through life without coming into direct conflict with Satan and his forces. And what is more unrealistic is to think that many (not all) of the problems which confront us day by day have no devilish strategy behind them. Satan is responsible for more of our troubles and difficulties than we may believe. The late Dr Martyn Lloyd-Jones said: "I am certain that one of the main causes of the ill state of the church today is the fact that the devil is being forgotten ... we have become so psychological in our attitude and thinking. We are ignorant of this great objective fact – the being, the existence of the devil, the adversary, the accuser and his 'fiery darts'."

Does the thought of doing battle with the devil frighten you? Then heed the words of Corrie ten Boom who said: "The fear of the devil is most likely from the devil himself." God has given us all the protection we need to defend ourselves against the attacks of Satan, and when we know how to avail ourselves of this protection, we will no longer be afraid of the devil – rather, he will be afraid of us.

When we know how to protect ourselves the devil will be afraid of us.

O God, as I go deeper into this subject, I am becoming increasingly aware of the intensity of the spiritual battle in which I am engaged. Dispel every fear that may arise within me and show me the way to power and victory. In Jesus' Name I pray. Amen.

OUR ONLY PROTECTION

For Reading and Meditation: Ephesians 6:11–18

"Put on the whole armour of God, that you may be able to stand against the wiles of the devil." (v. 11, NKJ)

We come now to focus our attention on the six separate sections of the spiritual armour which God has provided for us in Christ, but before we do we must pause to make clear a couple of important points. One, the armour of God is our only protection against the wiles of Satan, and two, it will do us no good unless we avail ourselves of it in its entirety.

A FALSE SECURITY

Today we concentrate on the first of these two vital issues. We must constantly keep before us the fact that such is the might and power of Satan that nothing apart from the armour of God will protect us from his onslaughts. Mark that and mark it well, for there are many Christians who have tried to stand against Satan in their own strength and have found themselves not victors, but victims. One of the "wiles" of Satan is to get us to believe that we can resist him in our own strength, but when we think that – we are finished.

In my time I have seen many believers lulled by Satan into thinking that their long experience in the faith and their understanding of Christian doctrine were all they needed to protect them from satanic attack, but they found to their cost that this was inadequate and insufficient. We never live more dangerously than when we depend on our spiritual experience and understanding to protect us from the fiery darts of the enemy. One thing and one thing only can protect us from the attacks of Satan and that is the spiritual armour which God has provided. You see, in the devil we are dealing with a foe that is inferior in power only to the Almighty Himself. Therefore, nothing less than the protection that God provides is adequate for our need.

The devil is inferior in power only to God therefore we need God's armour.

O Father, I need to get this matter straight, for I see that if my dependence is on anything other than You, then I am sunk. Drive this truth deep into my spirit this day. In Jesus' Name. Amen.

THE WHOLE ARMOUR OF GOD

For Reading and Meditation: Romans 13:8–14

"... So let us put aside the deeds of darkness and put on the armour of light." (v. 12)

Now we are clear that only the armour of God can give us the protection we need against the wiles of Satan, we must remind ourselves also that it will not do us any good unless it is worn in its entirety. We are exhorted to put on the whole armour of God – not just a few of the pieces we think are most suitable for us.

THE ESSENTIAL ARMOUR

This again is something of crucial importance. It means we are not to pick and choose in this matter. If we are to be steadfast soldiers in the Lord's army, if we are to avoid becoming what John Stott calls "wobbly Christians who have no firm foothold in Christ", then we must put on the entire equipment which God provides for us. We cannot, we dare not select parts of the armour and say, "I don't really like the helmet of salvation, but I don't mind wearing the breastplate of righteousness." You can do that, of course, but if you do then you must know exactly what will happen to you – you will be overcome by Satan. The moment you say, "I need the breastplate, but I don't need the helmet" – you are defeated. You need it all – the *whole* armour of God.

You see, our understanding of what is involved in spiritual defence against Satan is extremely inadequate – we just don't have sufficient knowledge of what is involved. It is God alone who knows our enemy and it is God alone who knows exactly how to protect us so that we remain firm and steadfast when Satan and his forces hurl themselves against us. So learn this lesson now before going any farther – every single piece of God's armour is essential, and to select some and leave the others is to take the route to failure and defeat.

God alone knows our enemy and God alone knows exactly how to protect us.

O God, deliver me from the attitude of pride that seeks to put my ideas ahead of Your ideas. You know more about what I need to protect me from the enemy than I do. Help me ever to trust Your judgement. In Jesus' Name I ask it. Amen.

THE BELT OF TRUTH

For Reading and Meditation: Psalm 119:145–160

"You are near, O Lord, And all your commandments are truth." (v. 151, NKJ)

Paul, in listing the six main pieces of a soldier's equipment, does so in order to illustrate the six main ways by which we can defend ourselves against the power of Satan – truth, righteousness, steadfastness, faith, salvation and the Word of God. Most commentators believe that the reason why Paul selected these six pieces of a soldier's armour to illustrate the Christian's protective system against satanic attack was because he was chained to one as he wrote the letter (Ephesians 6:20). And although it is unlikely that the soldier would have worn the full armour of an infantryman on the battlefield, the sight of him would have kindled Paul's imagination.

THE STRATEGIC ORDER

The list begins with the belt of truth. Why, we ask ourselves, does the apostle start with such a seemingly insignificant item? Why did he not begin with one of the bigger and more important pieces of equipment, such as the breastplate, the shield or the sword of the Spirit? The order in which these pieces are given to us is an inspired order, and if we change the order we make our position extremely perilous. For example, the reason why many Christians fail to wield the sword of the Spirit effectively is because they have not first girded their waist with truth. If we reverse the order, we succeed only in weakening our spiritual defence.

It is very important that we grasp this. Girding our waist with truth is always the place to start whenever we are under satanic attack. If you don't start right, then you will not finish right. So let this thought take hold of you: you cannot do battle with the devil until you first gird your waist with truth.

If we do not start with the belt of truth we weaken our spiritual defence.

Gracious and loving Father, help me to absorb this thought into my inner being this day so that it will stay with me for the rest of my life: I cannot do battle with the devil until I first gird my waist with truth. Amen.

THE POWER OF TRUTH

For Reading and Meditation: Psalm 51:1–17

"Surely you desire truth in the inner parts ..." (v. 6)

We ended yesterday by saying that we cannot do battle with the devil until we have first girded our waist with truth. Girding the waist was always a symbol of readiness to fight. That is why this comes first. The officers in the Roman army wore short skirts, very much like a Scottish kilt. Over this they had a cloak or tunic which was secured at the waist with a girdle. When they were about to enter into battle, they would tuck the tunic up under the girdle so as to leave their legs free and unencumbered for the fight.

TRUTH IN THE INNER BEING

We must now ask ourselves: What does Paul's phrase "gird your waist with truth" (Ephesians 6:14, NKJ) really mean? What significance or application does it have for us right here in the twentieth century? The word "truth" can be looked at in two ways: one, objective truth, as it is to be found in Jesus Christ, and two, subjective truth as it is to be found in the qualities of honesty and sincerity. The Puritan, William Gurnall, points out that whether the word implies truth of doctrine or truth of heart, one will not do without the other.

I personally believe that in Ephesians 6, Paul is empha-sising subjective truth – truth in the inner being. You see, when we are deceitful or hypocritical, or resort to intrigue and scheming, we are playing the devil's game. And believe me, you will never be able to beat the devil at his own game! What Satan despises and dislikes is transparent truth – he flees from it as quickly as darkness runs from the dawn. Having our waist girded with truth, then, means being pos-sessed with truth, guided by truth and controlled by truth. No truth – no power over Satan. It is as simple as that.

Satan flees from transparent truth as quickly as darkness runs from the dawn.

O Father, I see that You have set standards by which I rise or fall. When I fulfil them I rise, when I break them I fall. Give me the strength I need to fulfil all Your laws, especially the law of truth. In Jesus' Name. Amen.

THE SEARCHLIGHT OF TRUTH

Reading and Meditation: Psalm 139:1–24

*"Search me [thoroughly], O God, and know my heart!
Try me, and know my thoughts!" (v. 23, Amplified Bible)*

We remind ourselves of what we said yesterday – that to have our "waist girded with truth" means to be possessed by truth, to be willing for truth to govern and regulate every part of our lives. If we are to defend ourselves effectively against the attacks of Satan, then truth and honesty are vital necessities.

The mental health experts tell us that being willing to face the truth about ourselves is an important part of our growth toward maturity; the same is true in the realm of the spiritual. How easy it is to hide from the truth and imagine ourselves to be truthful when really we are not. Whatever his personal idiosyncrasies and his rebellious attitude toward Christianity, Sigmund Freud made an interesting contribution to our understanding of human personality when he documented with true genius the incredibly subtle ways in which we lie to ourselves. Psychologists call them "defence mechanisms", but a more Biblical view of them would be "lying mechanisms".

SELF-DECEPTION

We would all much prefer to be called defensive than dishonest. But whenever we allow ourselves to be self-deceived, we not only impede our spiritual growth – we also lower our defences against Satan. He thrives on deception, and if he can push us toward self-deception, he maintains a definite advantage over us. Many of us might react with horror to the suggestion that we may be dishonest, for we would not dream of doing or saying anything that was not according to truth. Yet it is possible to be open and honest on the outside and yet hide from truth on the inside. All of us, even mature and experienced Christians, are capable of hiding from truth.

Satan thrives on deception.

O Father, I see that if I am to overcome Satan, then I must know truth inwardly as well as outwardly. Search my heart today, dear Lord, and bring to the surface the things within me that are untrue. In Jesus' Name I ask it. Amen.

THREE FORMS OF DISHONESTY

For Reading and Meditation: I John 1:1–10

"If we claim to be without sin, we deceive ourselves and the truth is not in us." (v. 8)

The suggestion made yesterday that even experienced and mature Christians can inwardly resist truth, might surprise and shock some, but the real issue is this — is it true? Let me identify three of the most popular defences we use to resist truth, ones that almost all of us use from time to time.

PROJECTION

The first is projection. This is where we are to blame for something, but we project the blame on to someone else so that we feel more comfortable about ourselves. It may sound a simple thing, but all dishonesty deprives — even simple dishonesty.

DENIAL

Then take the defence of denial. How many times do we refuse to face the fact that we may be angry about something, and when someone says "Why are you angry?" we reply with bristling hostility: "I'm not angry!" We fail to recognise what others can plainly see. And denial, no matter how one looks at it, is a form of inner deceit and dishonesty.

RATIONALISATION

Another dishonest defence is rationalisation. We do this whenever we persuade ourselves that something is what it is not. C. S. Lewis points out in his writings that when our neighbour does something wrong, it is obviously because he or she is "bad", while if we do something wrong it is only because we did not get enough sleep, or someone gave us a rough time, or our blood chemistry is at fault, and so on.

All defence mechanisms deprive us of inner honesty, and apart from hindering our spiritual growth (as we said) they lower our defences against Satan. This is why over and over again in Scripture we are bidden to open up to honesty. The more honest we can be, the more spiritually powerful and effective we can be.

The more honest we can be, the more spiritually effective we can be.

Lord Jesus, help me to open up to honesty. For I see that the more honest I am, the more authority I can wield over Satan. I want to be able to say, as You said: "The ruler of this world is coming, and he has nothing in me." For Your own dear Name's sake. Amen.

DISHONESTY DISABLES

For Reading and Meditation: Hosea 10:12

"... it is time to seek the Lord ..."

The phrase "gird your waist with truth" clearly suggests that this is something we must do and not expect God to do for us. Clinton McLemore says: "Whenever any one of us embodies and promotes personal honesty, we are knowingly or unknowingly doing God's work." So ask yourself right now: "Am I an honest person?" If there are areas of your life where you are not sure, then spend some time before God in prayer today asking Him to help you root out all dishonesty and insincerity. For honesty is our first line of defence against Satan. If we are not honest, or not willing to be honest, then the devil will soon disable us.

EVASION OF THE TRUTH

We live in an age which, generally speaking, evades the truth. We seem to take it for granted that advertisements distort, contracts contain fine print that no one draws our attention to, and professionals conceal one another's malpractice. There are few domains of life that are uncompromised, few social structures that are not tainted, few relationships that retain any semblance of honesty and wholeness.

The Christian Church is not without blame either. Consider the endless and often angular manoeuvrings of some church boards and committees. God put the Church in the world but somehow the devil has put the world in the Church. Our text for today sums up the present Church situation: "It is time to seek the Lord." Am I speaking too strongly? I think not. If we don't get things straightened out at the start, then how can we hope to be victorious in the war against Satan? Always remember that sin, at its root, is a stubborn refusal to deal with truth.

Honesty is our first line of defence against Satan.

O God, forgive us that we, Your redeemed people, sometimes pursue our own interests and allow truth to be dragged in the gutter. Help us, dear Lord. For without truth we have no power. In Jesus' Name we ask it. Amen.

THE BREASTPLATE OF RIGHTEOUSNESS

For Reading and Meditation: Psalm 132:1–18

*"May your priests be clothed with righteousness;
may your saints sing for joy." (v. 9)*

W e look now at the second piece of armour with which we are to defend ourselves against the wiles of the devil – the breastplate of righteousness. A soldier's breastplate generally extended from the base of the neck to the upper part of the thighs, so it would cover many important parts of the body, in particular the heart.

FACE-TO-FACE COMBAT?

Some commentators are of the opinion that the word "breastplate" suggests that this piece of equipment covered only the front of the chest and thus no protection was provided for the soldier's back. They deduce from this that a Christian should face the devil and never turn his back on him or otherwise he will expose a part that is unguarded. It is an interesting idea but it must not be given too much credence, as the soldier's breastplate often covered his back as well as his front.

GUARDING THE HEART

What spiritual lesson and application can we draw from the "breastplate of righteousness"? Most commentators believe that because a soldier's breastplate covered mainly his heart, the spiritual application of this is that in Christ we have all the protection we need against negative or desolating feelings – the heart being seen as the focal point of the emotions. What an exciting thought is presented by this – by putting on the breastplate of righteousness, we have the resources to deal with all those debilitating feelings that tend to bring us down into depression and despair – unworthiness, inadequacy, fear, and so on. When I once mentioned this to a friend who asked me what I thought the breastplate of righteousness was for, he said: "It sounds too good to be true." I replied: "It's too good not to be true."

*In Christ
we have
protection
against
negative or
desolating
feelings.*

Gracious Lord and Master, how can I sufficiently thank You for providing a defence against this most difficult of problems – emotional distress. Show me how to apply Your truth to this part of my personality. In Jesus' Name. Amen.

ON CHRIST WE REST OUR CASE

For Reading and Meditation: Romans 8:31–39

"Who then will condemn us? Will Christ? No!
For he is the one who died for us ..." (v. 34, TLB)

Today we face the question: When Paul talks about the "breastplate of righteousness", is he talking about our righteousness or Christ's righteousness? I believe he is talking about Christ's righteousness. That is not to say, of course, that our own righteousness (or moral uprightness) is unimportant, for as Paul points out in 2 Corinthians 6:7, our personal righteousness can be a definite defence against Satan. In Ephesians 6, however, the emphasis is not on our righteousness in Christ, but Christ's righteousness in us.

CHRIST'S RIGHTEOUSNESS

So how does putting on the breastplate of righteousness act as a spiritual defence against the wiles of the devil? Take, for example, those people who have definitely surrendered their lives to Christ but whom Satan afflicts with a feeling that they are not good enough to be saved. Why do they have such feelings? The answer is simple – they have taken their eyes off Christ and His righteousness and have focused on themselves and their righteousness. And in doing that, they play right into the devil's hands.

You see, the devil can find all kinds of flaws and blemishes in your righteousness, but he can find nothing wrong with the righteousness of Christ. The way to withstand an attack like this is to put on the breastplate of righteousness. In other words, remind yourself and Satan that you stand, not on your own merits but on Christ's. This may sound simple, even simplistic to some, but I have lived long enough to see people latch on to it and come from the depths of emotional distress to the heights of spiritual exaltation.

Remind Satan you stand on Christ's merits.

Lord Jesus, help me to latch on to it too. Make it crystal clear to my spirit that although the devil can find many flaws in my righteousness, he cannot find a single flaw in Yours. I rest my case – on You. Thank You, dear Lord. Amen.

"THE TYRANNY OF THE OUGHTS"

For Reading and Meditation: Romans 5:1–11

"Therefore, since we have been justified through faith, we have peace with God through our Lord Jesus Christ." (v. 1)

We looked yesterday at how the breastplate of righteousness protects us from the feeling that we are not good enough to be saved. Today we look at another feeling which Satan delights to whip up in the heart of a Christian – the feeling that we are only accepted by God when we are doing everything perfectly.

PERFECTIONISM

This feeling gives rise to the condition known as perfectionism – a condition which afflicts multitudes of Christians.

The chief characteristic of perfectionism is a constant overall feeling of never doing enough to be thought well of by God. Karen Horney describes it as "the tyranny of the oughts". Here are some typical statements of those who are afflicted in this way: "I ought to do better", "I ought to have done better", "I ought to be able to do better". There is nothing wrong with wanting to do better, but in the twisted thinking of a perfectionist, he or she believes that because they could or ought to have done better, they will not be accepted or thought well of by God. They come to believe that their acceptance by God depends on their performance; they constantly try to develop a righteousness of their own rather than resting in the righteousness which Christ has provided for them.

If you suffer from this condition, then it's time to put on your spiritual breastplate. You need to remind yourself that the way you came into the Christian life is the way you go on in it – by depending on Christ and His righteousness, not on yourself and your righteousness. You are not working to be saved; you are working because you are saved.

You are not working to be saved; you are working because you are saved.

Lord Jesus, I see that when I stand in Your righteousness, I stand in God's smile. But when I stand in my own righteousness, I stand in God's frown. Help me move over from frown to smile. In Your dear Name. Amen.

PAUL'S BREASTPLATE IN PLACE

For Reading and Meditation: 1 Corinthians 15:1–11

"But by the grace of God I am what I am ..." (v. 10)

Another feeling which Satan can arouse in a heart that is unprotected by a spiritual breastplate is that of discouragement. I am thinking here not so much of the discouragement which comes directly from Satan, but a more subtle form of attack in which he draws our attention to what other Christians may be saying or thinking about us.

FACING CRITICISM

The apostle Paul was a particular target of Satan in this respect, but see how he used the breastplate of righteousness as his spiritual defence. Paul's background was anti-Christian and he could never get completely away from that. He had been the most hostile and brutal persecutor of the Church, and he must therefore have often met families whose loved ones had died because of him. Some might even have doubted his claim to be an apostle. We can't be sure about that, of course, but some commentators claim that in 1 Corinthians 15:9, he was replying to such an accusation.

CONFIDENT IN CHRIST

How does Paul react to the criticism? Does he succumb to discouragement? Does he say: "What's the use of working my fingers to the bone for these unappreciative people? They don't do anything but hurl recriminations in my face!" This is what the devil would have liked him to do. But look at what he does. He says: "By the grace of God I am what I am." Can you see what he is doing? He is using the breastplate of righteousness. He is saying, in other words: "I don't need to do anything to protect myself; what I am is what Christ has made me. I am not standing in my own righteousness, I am standing in His." What a lesson in how to use the spiritual breastplate. You and I need to learn this lesson too.

We are what Christ has made us.

O God, day by day I am catching little glimpses of what You are trying to teach me – that the more I depend on Your righteousness and the less I depend on my own, the better off I will be. Help me to learn it – and learn it completely. Amen.

HOW TO HANDLE CONFUSION

For Reading and Meditation: Romans 8:29–39

"... nothing will ever be able to separate us from the love of God demonstrated by our Lord Jesus Christ ..." (v. 39, TLB)

We look at yet another feeling which Satan delights to arouse in a heart that is unprotected by a spiritual breastplate – the feeling of confusion. None of us likes confusion because it erodes our sense of competence. Satan, knowing this, steps in whenever he can to take full advantage of it. Deep in the centre of our being is a compulsive demand to be in control, and to satisfy that demand we have to live in a predictable, understandable world. Confusion presents a serious challenge to our desire for control and is the enemy of those who like to have clear answers for everything.

UNANSWERED QUESTIONS

Whenever Satan sees that we are not wearing our spiritual breastplate, he comes to us and says something like this: "Look at the great problems that are all around you – earthquakes, famines, violence, cruelty to children ... how can you believe in a God of love when these things are going on in the world?" Sometimes he presses home these arguments with such power and force that you scarcely know where you are or how to answer. You cannot make sense of it, you cannot understand and you have no clear answers.

PEACE IN PERPLEXITY

The God who saved you must have your highest interests at heart.

There is only one protection against such assaults; it is to put on the breastplate of righteousness. You cannot understand particular happenings, you cannot give any explanation, but you do know that the God who clothed you with His righteousness and saved you from a lost eternity must have your highest interests and those of His universe at heart. When you hold on to that, your heart is protected from despair, even though your mind struggles to comprehend what is happening. You can live in peace even though you do not know all the answers.

Father God, I see that I can experience security in my heart even when my mind cannot understand Your ways. Hidden in Christ and His righteousness, I am safe. I am so thankful. Amen.

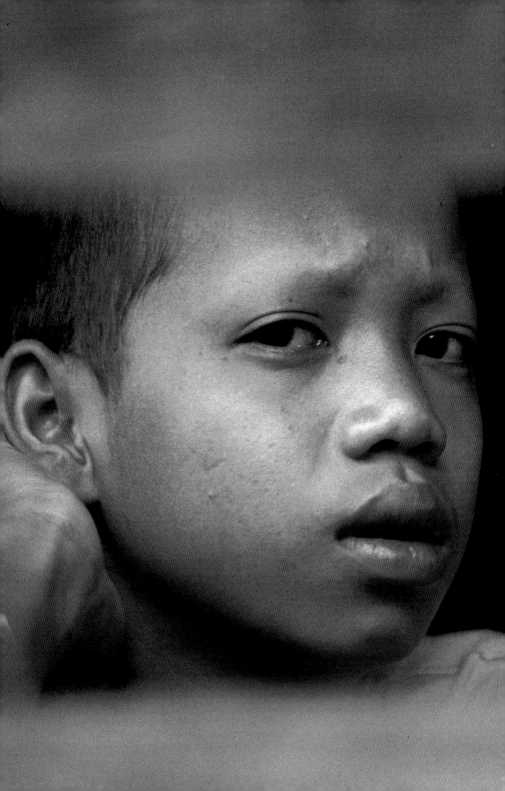

SATAN AS AN ANGEL OF LIGHT
For Reading and Meditation: Philippians 1:1–11

"... he who began a good work in you will carry it on to completion ..." (v. 6)

Yet another feeling which the devil delights to arouse in an unprotected and unguarded heart is the feeling that God does not love us. He times his attack to coincide with those moments when everything is going wrong and we are beset by all kinds of difficulties and problems. Then he moves alongside and whispers in our ear: "Do you still believe that God is love?" And when you respond by saying that you do, he transforms himself into an angel of light and tries another tactic: "Well," he says, "you may not be able to deny that God is love, but it is obvious that He does not love you, for if He did then He would not allow you to go through these difficult situations you are experiencing at the moment."

CERTAIN AND SECURE
Again, there is only one protection against such an assault; it is to put firmly in place the breastplate of righteousness. Nothing else will avail at this point. You must point him to the truth of Romans 8:28 – "We know that in all things God works for the good of those who love him." Notice, Paul does not say, "we understand", but "we know that in all things God works for the good of those who love him, who have been called according to his purpose."

This brings you directly to the theme of justification by faith, which is in fact the righteousness of Christ. You rest on that, and that is all you need. You must say to yourself: "He would never have clothed me with His righteousness if He had not set His love upon me and saved me. I will have courage. I do not know what is happening to me now. I cannot fathom it. But if He has begun His work in me, then I know He will go on to complete it."

If God has begun His work in us, He will go on to complete it.

O God, what wondrous power there is in Your Word. I can feel it doing me good even as I read and ponder it. Give me a greater knowledge of Your Word, for only through that can I maintain an advantage over the devil. In Jesus' Name. Amen.

WHAT HAPPENS WHEN WE SIN?

For Reading and Meditation: 1 John 1:5–10 & 2:1–2

"If we confess our sins, he is faithful and just and will forgive us our sins and purify us from all unrighteousness." (v. 9)

We look finally at another feeling which the devil likes to arouse in an unguarded and unprotected heart – the feeling that when we have committed a sin, we will be rejected by God and have to forfeit our salvation. You are probably aware that the Hebrew name "Satan" means "adversary" and the Greek name for "devil" means "slanderer". This gives us a pretty good idea of the nature of the Evil One – he is never happier than when he is engaged in pointing the finger of scorn and accusation at us whenever we have sinned or failed.

FALLIBLE BUT FORGIVEN

It is part of the doctrine of the Church that a Christian may sometimes fall into sin. We are saved, but we are still fallible. God forbid that we should fall into sin, but when we do, we must remember that we have "an advocate with the Father, Jesus Christ the righteous" (1 John 2:1, AV). You can be sure, however, that when you fall into sin, the devil will come to you and say: "You were forgiven when you became a Christian because you sinned in ignorance, but now that you are a Christian you have sinned against the light. There can be no forgiveness for you now. You are lost – and lost for ever."

The answer to this, as with all of Satan's accusations, is to put on the breastplate of righteousness. You must remind him that God's righteousness not only covers us at our salvation but continues to cover us for time and eternity. Never allow the devil to use a particular sin to call into question your whole standing before God. That is something that has been settled in heaven, not in the debating chamber of the devil.

God's righteousness covers us for time and eternity.

My Father and my God, my heart overflows at the revelation of Your full and free forgiveness. Help me not to take it for granted but to take it with gratitude. In Jesus' Name I pray. Amen.

THE SHOES OF PEACE

For Reading and Meditation: Philippians 1:12–30

"… stand firm in one spirit, contending as one man for the faith of the gospel." (v. 27)

We come now to the third piece of armour – having our "feet shod with the preparation of the gospel of peace" (Ephesians 6:15, AV). Shoes are absolutely essential to a soldier. Imagine an infantryman clad in armour but with no shoes on – a barefoot soldier. The rough ground would tear his feet to pieces and would soon render him unfit for duty. But with a stout pair of shoes, he would be ready to face anything that came.

A FIRM FOOTING

Markus Barth, a Bible commentator, says that the shoes which a Roman soldier would have worn in Paul's day were not so much a shoe as a sandal. They were known as *caligae* (half boots) which consisted of "heavy studded leather soles and were tied to the ankles or shins with more or less ornamental straps". These equipped the soldier for a solid stance and prevented his feet from slipping or sliding.

What is the spiritual application of all this? What did the apostle Paul have in mind when he penned the words: "Stand therefore, having … your feet shod with the preparation of the gospel of peace"? The New English Bible brings home the point of the passage in a most effective way when it translates it thus: "Let the shoes on your feet be the gospel of peace, to give you firm footing." The shoes we are to put on are the gospel of peace – the tried and tested truths of the Gospel – and their purpose is to prevent us from slipping and sliding when we do battle with our wily and nimble adversary, the devil. What are you like when under attack from Satan? Firm and resolute – or unsteady and unsure?

We need a firm stance to do battle with our wily, nimble adversary.

O Father, I see that if I am to stand firm and resolute when under enemy attack, my feet must be securely shod. Show me what is expected of me, dear Lord – and help me apply it. In Jesus' Name I pray. Amen.

THE IRREDUCIBLE MINIMUM

For Reading and Meditation: 2 Corinthians 1:12–24

"For no matter how many promises God has made, they are 'Yes' in Christ ..." (v. 19)

It is time now to face some very personal and pointed questions. Some may have difficulty in facing these questions but I would urge you to do so nevertheless. Do you believe the Bible is the Word of God, divinely and uniquely inspired and reliable in all it affirms? Do you believe that Jesus Christ is the Son of God, born of a virgin, and the only way to God? Do you believe that He was crucified for your sins, raised again on the third day and is now sitting on the right hand of God?

BASIC BELIEFS

I could go on raising more and more questions but the ones I have mentioned are what I consider to be the irreducible minimum of Christianity. In other words, these are the basic truths of the Gospel and if you don't take your stand on these truths, then you cannot call yourself a Christian. This is what is meant by having your feet shod with the preparation of the gospel of peace – you are ready to stand for the authority of Scripture, the deity of Christ, His substitutionary death, His resurrection from the dead and His return to earth in power and glory.

Do you know where you stand on these matters? Are you sure of your spiritual position? How can you fight the enemy if you do not know what you believe? As I write, some of the daily newspapers here in Britain are calling on church leaders to give a spiritual lead. But many of our leaders do not have a high view of Scripture. How can they give a lead when they don't know where they are going? They don't know where they stand and no one else knows either.

You cannot fight the enemy if you do not know what you believe.

O Father, Your Word promises to be a lamp to our feet and a light for our path. Bring those whose feet are slipping and sliding in the faith back to an unshakeable confidence in the Gospel. In Jesus' Name I ask it. Amen.

A Spiritual Adventure

For Reading and Meditation: Judges 7:1–22

"The Lord said to Gideon, 'With the three hundred men that lapped I will save you ...'" (v. 7)

I have selected this passage today because it illustrates the point I have been making, namely, that God is looking for people who will "stand". When the hosts of Midian came against the Israelites, Gideon gathered together a large army of 32,000 men. Then God reduced them to a mere handful. Of the 32,000, there were only 300 whom God could trust. He saw that they were men who would stand and never quit, so He dismissed the rest and with just a small army of 300 proceeded to discomfort and rout the Midianites.

Eligibility for call-up

God has always done His greatest work in and through a comparatively small number of people. When it comes to spiritual victories, forget the idea of numbers – what God wants is men and women who are prepared to stand, whose feet are "shod with the preparation of the gospel of peace". He will not entrust great responsibility to people whom He knows will not stand, for that would be an exercise in fruitlessness.

Are you standing for God – in your place of work, your home or the environment in which God has put you? Have you been in the Christian life for just a short time? Now that you are a Christian, take your stand unflinchingly on the Lord's side. But you cannot stand until you are prepared to stand. It begins with a firm and resolute attitude which then issues in firm and resolute action. As in Gideon's day, the Lord is looking for men and women who will take their stand on His Word, come what may, and commit themselves to doing what He asks even though they may not feel like it or see the sense of it. Are you such a one? If you are, then I predict that ahead of you is an exciting spiritual adventure.

A firm and resolute attitude issues in firm and resolute action.

O God, help me not to miss the highest because of my spiritual unpreparedness. Help me to be ready for all that You have for me – even before I see it. In Jesus' Name I pray. Amen.

PEACE THAT DOES NOT GO TO PIECES
For Reading and Meditation: Colossians 3:1–17

"... let the peace of God rule in your hearts ..." (v. 15, NKJ)

O ver the past few days we have been building up a picture of what it means to have our "feet shod with the preparation of the gospel of peace". One question remains – why the phrase "the gospel of peace"? Well, the Gospel is first and foremost a message about peace. First we experience peace with God, and then we experience the peace of God.

MATTERS OF CONCERN
A soldier in battle has to be certain about a number of things or else he will be distracted and become an easy prey for the enemy. He needs to be certain that he is fighting in a just war, that his commander is a wise strategist and that he has the constant support of those under whose authority he fights. He needs to know also that his loved ones are being cared for and that they are being protected by a defence force. It is the same with a Christian soldier. He too has to be certain about a number of things – his relationship with God, the truth and reliability of the Bible, the resources that are available to him, and so on. How can his heart be at peace if he is not assured of these things?

INSIDE INFORMATION
It is precisely at this point that we Christians have an advantage over every other soldier, for not only are we led by the wisest military strategist in the universe, but we have inside information on how the battle against Satan will end – we win! We would never be able to stand against the wiles of the devil unless we enjoyed peace with God and the peace of God. Even in the midst of the hottest conflict, we know that although the devil may win some of the battles, he will most definitely lose the war. If you have peace about the outcome, then you have peace all the way – period.

If you have peace about the outcome, then you have peace all the way.

O Father, I see so clearly that if I have doubts about You or about my salvation, then I will not be able to fight the enemy. I shall have to spend the whole time struggling with myself. But there are no doubts. I have peace with You and peace within. I am so thankful. Amen.

THE SHIELD OF FAITH

For Reading and Meditation: I John 5:1–12

"... This is the victory that has overcome the world, even our faith." (v. 4)

We come now to the fourth piece of equipment in the Christian soldier's armoury – the shield of faith: "Above all," says the apostle, "taking the shield of faith with which you will be able to quench all the fiery darts of the wicked one" (Ephesians 6:16, NKJ).

DESIGNED FOR A PURPOSE

Note two important facts, the first being Paul's use of the expression "above all". Some take this to mean, "above everything else in importance", and from this, they go on to argue that the last three pieces of armour are more important than the first three. But the phrase really means "in addition to these", and should not be seen as comparing one section of the armour with another. It is a transition phrase designed to introduce us to a section of the armour which has a different point and purpose.

The second fact is this – the six pieces of armour fall clearly into two main groups, the first consisting of the belt of truth, the breastplate of righteousness and the shoes of the preparation of the gospel of peace. The second group comprises the shield of faith, the helmet of salvation and the sword of the Spirit. The first three pieces of armour were fixed to the body by a special fastening, and hence, to a certain degree – immovable. But with the next three, there is a difference. The shield was not fixed to the body; it was something quite separate. The same applies to the helmet; that, too, was something that could be put on or taken off quite easily. And obviously the same was true of the sword of the Spirit. The lesson, quite clearly, is this – the first three pieces of equipment should be worn at all times, while the other three are to be taken up when and where it is necessary.

Wear the belt, breast-plate and shoes at all times; use the shield, helmet and sword when necessary.

Gracious and loving heavenly Father, I am so thankful for the care and design that has gone into providing for me a sure defence against Satan. I have learned much, yet I see there is still much more to learn. Teach me, my Father. Amen.

"FIERY DARTS"
For Reading and Meditation: 2 Timothy 4:1–18

"... the Lord stood at my side and gave me strength ... And I was delivered from the lion's mouth." (v. 17)

The main purpose of the shield in Roman times was to protect the soldiers from the fiery darts that would be thrown at them by the enemy. These fiery darts, made either of wood or metal, were covered with inflammable material and set alight immediately before being thrown. Enemies would throw these at each other in great numbers and from all directions so as to produce confusion and distraction. When attacked in this way, a soldier would hold up the shield in front of him, allowing the fiery darts to land on the fireproof metal surface, from which they would drop away harmlessly.

UNDERSTANDING THE ONSLAUGHT

The apostle says that we Christians, too, need a shield – a "shield of faith" – in order "to quench all the fiery darts of the wicked one" (Ephesians 6:16, NKJ). An understanding of what these "fiery darts" are is essential if we are to stand firm against the adversary. Have you ever gone to bed at night feeling perfectly happy and content, only to wake in a sad and melancholy mood? If there was no obvious physical or psychological reason for that, the chances are that you have experienced one of Satan's "fiery darts".

Sometimes they come as evil thoughts, even blasphemous thoughts, which intrude suddenly into our thinking, often at the most incongruous times. We may be reading the Bible, we may be kneeling in prayer, when all of a sudden some filthy or lewd thought flashes into our mind. It is a "fiery dart" from the devil. The point you must see is this – they do not come from inside us but from outside us. They strike us. Some thoughts arise from within our carnal nature but these come from without – from Satan. And we are foolish if we do not recognise this and deal with them in this light.

To stand firm we must recognise and deal with the devil's "fiery darts".

O Father, help me to be alert and able to recognise the "fiery darts" of Satan when they are hurled at me. For I see that it is only when I recognise them that I can deal effectively with them. Give me insight and understanding. In Jesus' Name. Amen.

PROMPT ACTION

For Reading and Meditation: Romans 10:1–18

"... faith comes by hearing, and hearing by the word of God." (v. 17, NKJ)

We ended yesterday with a prayer for God to help us understand how to use the shield of faith when we need to defend ourselves against the "fiery darts" of the devil. Prayerfully, then, we ask ourselves the question – how does faith act as a protective shield?

WHAT IS FAITH?

First of all, we must understand what faith is and how the word is being used by Paul in Ephesians 6:16. A little boy, when asked to give a definition of faith, said: "Faith is believing something you know isn't true." Well, that is precisely what faith is not. Faith is believing what you know to be true. But it is even more than that – it is *acting* on what you know to be true. Some people see faith as something vague and mysterious, but faith is one of the most practical commodities in the Christian life. Take this verse, for example: "Faith without deeds is dead" (James 2:26). There is always the element of activity in faith; it always prompts us to action. The Old Testament heroes of Hebrews 11 have in common decisive action triggered by faith.

FAITH IN ACTION

Faith is acting on what you know to be true.

Taking the shield of faith, then, is responding to the things the devil hurls at us by the quick application of what we believe about God and His Word, the Bible. When Satan sends his "fiery darts" in our direction, we can either stand and lament the fact that we are being attacked, or quickly raise the shield of faith and remind ourselves that the devil is a liar from the very beginning, and because we are redeemed by the blood of Christ, he has no legal or moral right to taunt us. But believing that is not enough; it must be acted on – and acted on quickly.

Father, I see that when Satan throws his "fiery darts" at me I must act, and act quickly. Help my faith to be so strong that it will not need a "jump start" to get it going. This I ask in Jesus' Name. Amen.

THE HELMET OF SALVATION
For Reading and Meditation: 2 Corinthians 11:1–15

"... I am afraid that just as Eve was deceived by the serpent's cunning, your minds may somehow be led astray ..." (v. 3)

We come now to the second piece of armour which is not tied or fixed to the body but which a Christian soldier has to take up and put on – "the helmet of salvation" (Ephesians 6:17). The helmet worn by a Roman soldier was usually made of bronze or iron with an inside lining of felt or sponge. In some cases, a hinged visor added frontal protection. When a Roman soldier saw an enemy coming, he would take hold of his shield, put on his helmet, take his sword in hand and stand alert and ready to do battle.

STRAIGHT THINKING

The figure of a helmet immediately suggests to us that this is something designed to protect the mind, the intelligence, the ability to think and reason. Just as the breastplate of righteousness protects us from emotional distress, so the helmet of salvation protects us from mental distress. This helmet can help us keep our thinking straight and preserve us from mental confusion and darkness.

As you look out at the world, has there ever been a time when we needed something to keep our thinking straight more than we do now? Politicians vacillate and oscillate between despairing pessimism and unrealistic optimism. Just think of the staggering complexities of the issues we face in our generation – AIDS, violence, nuclear missiles, international tension, economic instability, inner city slums, and so on. The intelligentsia of our day confess to being utterly baffled in dealing with the problems with which human society is confronted. Where can we turn to ease the pressure on our minds? The only answer is God – and in the helmet of salvation which He provides.

The helmet of salvation protects us from mental distress.

O Father, I am so grateful that You have provided freedom from that most terrifying of human problems – mental distress. Teach me all I need to know in applying Your truth to the important area of my mind. In Jesus' Name. Amen.

THE TENSES OF SALVATION

For Reading and Meditation: I Thessalonians 5:1–11

"… let us be self-controlled, putting on faith and love as a breastplate, and the hope of salvation as a helmet." (v. 8)

We said yesterday that never has there been a time when we need to keep our thinking straight more than we do now. You can be sure that Satan will take advantage of every situation that comes his way to disable a Christian and he will not hesitate to use chaotic world conditions and problems to oppress the mind. God's answer to this is the helmet of salvation.

LOOKING TO THE FUTURE

It is important to realise that Paul is not talking here about the salvation of the soul. He is not referring to salvation as regeneration or conversion. This is the mistake that many make when attempting to interpret this verse. They say: "Whenever the devil attacks your mind and seeks to oppress it, remind yourself that you have been saved." Well, there is nothing wrong with that, of course, and this explanation is mistaken, not because it is untrue, but because it does not go far enough.

The best way to interpret a verse of Scripture is with another verse of Scripture. Thus the text before us today throws a shaft of light on Paul's statement in Ephesians 6:17, for it shows salvation, not just as something in the past but something that is also future. He uses the word in the same way in Romans when he says: "Our salvation is nearer now than when we first believed" (Romans 13:11).

In the Bible, the word "salvation" has three distinct tenses – past, present and future. At conversion, we are saved from the penalty of sin. Now, day by day, we are being saved from the power of sin. And one day in the future, we will be saved from the presence of sin. And it is to the future Paul is looking when he invites us to put on the helmet of salvation.

Salvation is past, present and future.

O Father, thank You for reminding me of the tenses of salvation. I see that in order to live effectively, I must view the present tense by the future tense. Help me lay hold on this. In Jesus' Name. Amen.

GOD'S ETERNAL PLAN

For Reading and Meditation: Romans 8:18–30

"For in this hope we were saved." (v. 24)

O ur passage today shows even more clearly what we were discussing yesterday – salvation in the future tense. What is Paul talking about in these verses? He is talking about the time when Christ will return, when the kingdom of God will be established and when creation will be delivered from its bondage. The helmet of salvation, therefore, is the recognition that all human schemes, all human disorder and all human chaos will one day be ended, and when that happens, the whole universe will see that God has been quietly working out His purposes in and through everything.

FALSE HOPE

That truth, when understood and embraced, is the one thing above all others that will enable us to keep our thinking straight in a world that is full of confusion and darkness. Why is it that thoughtful minds like H. G. Wells, Bernard Shaw and others were and are so bewildered by what they see in the world? It is because they pin their hopes on unreliable and unrealistic resources. As the Dean of Melbourne wrote about H. G. Wells: "He hailed science as a panacea for all ills and the goddess of knowledge and power."

But what were H. G. Wells' conclusions about the world before he died? He wrote this: "The science to which I pinned my faith is bankrupt. Its counsels, which should have established the millennium, led instead directly to the suicide of Europe. I believed them once. In their name I helped destroy the faith of millions of worshippers in the temples of a thousand creeds. And now they look at me and witness the great tragedy of an atheist who has lost his faith." There is no protection in the world for the mind.

Despite appearances to the contrary, God is working out His eternal plan.

Something, my Father, is being burned into my consciousness – there is just no hope outside of You. If I break with You I break with sanity. Help me to walk closely with You so that Your mind becomes my mind. In Jesus' Name. Amen.

EVERYTHING IS UNDER CONTROL

For Reading and Meditation: Ephesians 1:3–14

"... according to the plan of him who works out everything in conformity with the purpose of his will ..." (v. 11)

We are seeing that the salvation spoken of in the phrase, "the helmet of salvation", is not so much the salvation we are enjoying at the present but the salvation we are going to enjoy when God works out His eternal purposes. The Christian has a hope for the future; he has an understanding that God is working out His purposes in history and therefore we need not be disturbed when human programmes appear to be going wrong. We hear about "new deals" and "fair deals" and "better deals", yet they end up in disappointment for all concerned.

PROSPECTS FOR THE FUTURE

The Christian expects the world to get worse and worse, for that is what the Bible tells us will happen. He expects false teachings and false philosophies to abound. He expects the world's systems to fail, for anything that is not built on Christ has no guarantee of success. The Christian knows that wars and international tension are unavoidable, even though every effort should be made to avoid them. The world is in such a state and such a condition that the more attention we give it, the more weary our minds become.

What is a Christian to do in such a world as ours? How are we to react when the devil takes advantage of our sensitivity to world conditions and focuses our thoughts upon them? Shall we give up? Shall we withdraw from life? No, we put on the helmet of salvation and remind ourselves that in the face of everything that appears contrary, God is working out His eternal plan and purpose. History is His-story. The Almighty God is at work in the very events that appear to be filled with darkness and confusion.

History is His-story.

O God, help me see that although You are apart from the events of history, You are also in the events of history. Ultimately all things are going to glorify You. Thank You, Father. Amen.

"NOT A PRIVATE FIGHT"
For Reading and Meditation: 2 Chronicles 20:4–26

"... Do not be afraid or discouraged ... For the battle is not yours, but God's." (v. 15)

At the risk of being repetitive, let me spell out once again what I believe is the spiritual application of the helmet of salvation. It is not so much the enjoyment of our present salvation (though it includes that) but the assurance that a certain, sure salvation is coming and is even now at work.

You see, this is what we need to know if we are to prevent the devil from bringing us into a state of mental distress – not merely that things will finally end right but that God's plan is being worked out now. "History," writes Ray Stedman, an American Bible teacher, "is not a meaningless jumble but a controlled pattern, and the Lord Jesus Christ is the one who is directing these events." The attack of Satan on the mind proceeds along this line. He says: "Just look around you at the state of the world. God seems powerless to put things right. He has given lots of promises that things will one day get better, but none of those promises have come to pass. Hadn't you better give up this foolish idea that it's all going to work out right?"

A GUARANTEED OUTCOME
It you were to let your mind dwell on that kind of satanic argument, you would soon find yourself in distress. The answer is to put on the helmet, the hope of salvation. You must remind yourself that things are not as they appear. The battle is not ours, but the Lord's. This is not a private fight we are engaged in. We may be individual soldiers fighting in the army of God, but the ultimate cause is sure and the end is certain. We need not be unduly troubled by what is happening in the world – our Commander is not just winning; He has already won.

The battle is not ours, but the Lord's.

Lord Jesus, I am grateful that the cross is the guarantee that neither sin nor Satan will ever defeat You. Your victory at Calvary has settled for ever the question of who has the final word in the universe. I am so deeply, deeply thankful. Amen.

WE SEE JESUS

For Reading and Meditation: Hebrews 2:1–15

" ... we do not see everything subject to him. But we see Jesus ..." (vv. 8–9)

Are you troubled as you look out at the situation in the world? Well, according to the Bible things are going to get worse; as Jesus said, "Men's hearts failing them from fear and the expectation of those things which are coming on the earth" (Luke 21:26, NKJ).

A GLORIOUS HOPE

How are Christians going to stand when the darkness deepens and things get very much worse? What will we do when international tension increases, making it difficult for nation to communicate with nation? Christians have a glorious hope – the hope of salvation. It is this, and this alone, which enables believers to live out their lives free from mental distress. I am sure you have already discovered that after reading the morning newspaper, you move into the day feeling somewhat jaded and depressed. Why is this? It is because almost daily, our newspapers are filled with murder, rape, violence, economic distress, abortion and child abuse. And our conscience, which through conversion has been sensitised to the moral laws of God, begins to reverberate as it comes up against the reports of things we know are contrary to the divine principles.

Satan, seeing our concern, attempts to exploit it for his own ends. "Things are getting worse, aren't they?" he says. "Why don't you just admit that God has lost control of His world?" If we did not have the helmet of salvation to put on at such a moment, we would finish up with the same attitude as H. G. Wells, who after the Second World War, wrote: "The spectacle of evil in the world has come near to breaking my spirit." Again I say, there is no protection in the world for the mind.

Christians have a glorious hope – the hope of salvation.

My Father and my God, where would I be if I could not cling to a text such as that in my reading for today? My spirit too would be near to breaking. I am so thankful that in You there is hope – hope with a capital H. Amen.

THE WAY TO AN UNDISTURBED MIND
For Reading and Meditation: Colossians 1:9–28

"... Christ in you, the hope of glory." (v. 27)

Here in the land where I live, the British Isles, we are relatively free from much of what concerns and distresses others. We have much to be sad about but we have much to be glad about also. We can still preach the Gospel in our churches and can still enjoy freedom of speech. But I know that in some areas of the world Satan is openly worshipped and faith is not allowed to be expressed openly.

IN GOD WE HOPE
What do Christians living in these places do to prevent themselves from becoming wearied by their adverse conditions and circumstances? There is only one thing they can do – they must put on the helmet of the hope of salvation. This, more than anything, will help keep their thinking straight. But no matter where in the world we live, those of us who have enlisted in the army of God must do the same. We must not succumb to the popular delusion that the working out of all human problems lies just around the corner through the application of humanistic ideas and philosophies.

How long has the world grasped at this futile dream? Almost from the dawn of history, men and women have been grasping after the elusive hope that something can be worked out here. But God has never said that. Consistently throughout the Scriptures, He has said that man in his fallen condition is totally unable to work out his problems. We know, however, that He has reserved a day of salvation when all wrongs will be righted, and it is only in the strength of the hope of that day of salvation that our hearts and minds can be kept undisturbed.

On the day of salvation all wrongs will be righted.

O Father, how can I ever be grateful enough that I am caught up in an eternal purpose. I live in the present, yet I draw also from the certainties of the future. Nourish this hope within me until it drives out every fear. In Jesus' Name. Amen.

THE SWORD OF THE SPIRIT

For Reading and Meditation: James 4:1–10

"... Stand firm against the devil; resist him and he will flee from you." (v. 7, Amplified Bible)

We come now to the last of the six pieces in the Christian soldier's armour – "the sword of the Spirit, which is the word of God" (Ephesians 6:17). John Stott points out that "of all the six pieces of armour or weaponry listed, the sword is the only one which can clearly be used for attack as well as defence". And the kind of attack envisaged here is one that involves a close encounter, for the word used for sword is *machaira,* meaning a short sword or dagger.

COUNTER-ATTACK

As soon as we begin talking about the sword as being a weapon of attack, we see that there is much more to spiritual warfare than standing up to the devil – we have, according to our text today, the potential to make him "flee". The word "flee" is a very strong word in the original Greek. It means much more than a strategic withdrawal; it means beating a swift and hasty retreat. What an amazing truth! It is possible for a Christian so to resist the devil that he races away as fast as he can.

This truth must not be seen in any way as limiting the devil's power, for he is a strong and determined foe. It means rather that although he has great power and strength, a Christian able to wield the sword of the Spirit can ensure that he is overpowered and discomfited. We are right when we develop a healthy respect for the devil's wiles and ingenuity, but we are wrong when we allow him to terrorise and frighten us. We must have the assurance, given everywhere in the New Testament, that to engage in conflict with the devil is not a hopeless task. We are not to indulge in over-confidence but, at the same time, we are not to be terrorised or frightened by him.

A Christian can so resist the devil that he will flee.

O Father, the thought that I, a sinner saved by grace, am able to send Satan into retreat almost overwhelms me. Yet I must believe it, for Your Word tells me so. Help me understand even more clearly the authority I have in Christ. In His Name I ask it. Amen.

THE POWER OF PRECISE SCRIPTURE

For Reading and Meditation: Matthew 4:1–11

"... It is written ... It is also written ..."
(vv. 4 & 7)

We must focus now on what is meant by the phrase "the sword of the Spirit, which is the word of God". Some interpret it to mean that the Holy Spirit is the Word of God. But nowhere in the Bible is the Holy Spirit described as the Word of God. That description is confined solely to our Lord Jesus Christ. Well, if the Spirit is not the sword – what is? The sword is the Word of God, the Bible, the inspired Scriptures.

A READY REPLY

In the passage before us today we see a perfect illustration of how Jesus used the sword of the Spirit when rebutting the temptations of the devil. Notice how, prior to the temptation, Jesus was anointed by the Holy Spirit (Matthew 3:13–17). Next we are informed that Jesus was "led by the Spirit into the desert to be tempted by the devil" (4:1). During the temptation our Lord, filled with the Spirit, resisted every one of the devil's statements by using the precise words of Scripture. Follow me closely, for this is extremely important: Christ did not merely utter a newly formed statement or something that came to Him on the spur of the moment, but quoted a text which had already been given by God and written down. The weapon used by our Lord was the Word of God, the Scriptures.

Nothing defeats Satan more thoroughly than the Word of God.

Can you see the point I am making? Satan is not rebuffed by clever phrases that are made up on the spur of the moment and may sound theologically sophisticated and refined; he is defeated only when we quote to him the precise words of Scripture. If this was the strategy Jesus had to use, then how much more you and I. Nothing defeats Satan more thoroughly and effectively than the sword of the Spirit, which is the Word of God.

O God, open my eyes that I might see more clearly than ever the power and authority that lies in Your sacred Word, the Bible. Help me to know it better. For Your own dear Name's sake. Amen.

THE BIBLE – AN INSPIRED BOOK

For Reading and Meditation: John 16:1–15

"... when he, the Spirit of truth, comes, he will guide you into all truth." (v. 13)

Today we ask ourselves: Why are the Scriptures described as a sword provided by the Holy Spirit? It means, quite simply, that it is the Holy Spirit who has given us the Scriptures. They come altogether from Him. It was the Holy Spirit who inspired men to write them: "Men spoke from God as they were carried along by the Holy Spirit" (2 Peter 1:21). Again in 2 Timothy 3:16 we read: "All Scripture is God-breathed" – a statement which assures us that the Scriptures come from the Holy Spirit.

WITHOUT ERROR

The Bible is not a mere human document, the product of the mind of man. The Holy Spirit breathed into men and inspired them to write the way they did. This does not mean that the people who wrote the Scriptures did so mechanically, in the way that someone would dictate into a dictating machine. The Holy Spirit used their natural way of expression but gave them an additional ability to write without error. It is vital, if you are to win the battle against Satan, that you not only see this but believe it. When you consider how strong and powerful Satan is, then you need something that is even more strong and powerful. And the Bible, the inspired Word of God, is your strength.

We must, however, go one step further – only the Holy Spirit can enable us truly to understand God's Word: "We have not received the spirit of the world but the Spirit who is from God, that we may understand what God has freely given us" (1 Corinthians 2:12). Without the Holy Spirit, we would be no more able to understand the Scriptures than a blind man could judge a beauty contest.

Only the Holy Spirit can enable us truly to understand God's Word.

Gracious Holy Spirit, just as You breathed into the Bible to give it its life and power, breathe also into my heart today so that I might know and understand its truth. I ask this in Jesus' Name. Amen.

"DIVIDE AND CONQUER"

For Reading and Meditation: I Corinthians 2:1–16

"... the things that come from the Spirit of God ... are spiritually discerned." (v. 14)

W e ended yesterday with the thought that only the Holy Spirit can help us to understand the Word of God. I will go further and say that only the Holy Spirit can help us properly to interpret it. A man may have a fine mind, a good seminary training, even a theological degree, but that is not a sufficient foundation on which to attempt to interpret the Word of God. Truth, as our text for today tells us, is "spiritually discerned".

WORD AND SPIRIT

But there is one more thing we need to understand – only the Holy Spirit can show us how to use it aright. Doubtless this was the consideration in the mind of the apostle when he penned the statement we are considering: "the sword of the Spirit, which is the word of God". It is one thing to know the contents of Scripture; it is another thing to know how to use those contents in a way that defeats and over-comes the devil. Only the Holy Spirit can enable us to do this.

The relationship between the Holy Spirit and the Word of God is an important one. Some tend to put the emphasis on one side or the other. But the moment we separate the Spirit and the Word, we are in trouble. The late Donald Gee once said: "All Spirit and no Word, you blow up. All Word and no Spirit, you dry up. Word and Spirit – you grow up." Without the Spirit, the Word is a dead letter; with the Spirit, it is a living and powerful force. The devil has a policy of "divide and conquer", and if he can get us to separate the Word from the Spirit, then he has us just where he wants us.

With the Spirit, the Word of God is a living and powerful force.

My Father, I see that when I separate the Spirit from the Word and the Word from the Spirit, I am in trouble. Help me to be as open to the Spirit as I am to the Bible, and as open to the Bible as I am to the Spirit. In Jesus' Name. Amen.

THE DIVINE DESIGN
For Reading and Meditation: John 14:15–27

"... the Counsellor, the Holy Spirit ... will teach you all things and will remind you of everything I have said to you." (v. 26)

We said yesterday that only the Holy Spirit can enable us to use the contents of Scripture in a way that helps us to overcome and defeat the devil. How does this work out in practice?

A RECEPTIVE MIND

When we come to God's Word, laying aside all pre-conceived ideas and depending entirely on the Holy Spirit to reveal its truth to us, we put ourselves in a position where the Holy Spirit can impress the truth of the Scriptures into our innermost being. There it takes root within us, and whenever we stand in need of a word with which to rebut the devil, the Holy Spirit brings it to our remembrance.

THE SPIRIT'S ILLUMINATION

And here's the most wonderful thing – the Word of God on our lips will have the same effect upon the devil as if he was hearing it from the lips of Jesus Himself! Every time we open the Bible, we must be careful to pray for the help and illumination of the Spirit so that we don't finish up making the Bible mean what we want it to mean. When we do that, we are following the divine design – letting the Spirit bring home to our hearts the truth and meaning of His own Word.

This attitude of humility and receptivity gives the Holy Spirit the opportunity He needs to build the truth of the Word of God into our spirits. Approaching the Bible in this way, said the late J. B. Phillips, "is like rewiring a house where the electricity has not been turned off". You touch something that lets you know there is a current of power flowing through its pages that was not put there by any man. The Holy Spirit has gone into it, so is it any wonder that the Holy Spirit comes out of it?

A current of power flows through the pages of Scripture.

My Father and my God, I know the Spirit dwells in Your Word. I come now to ask that He might dwell also in me, to open up my whole being to the truth and power that lies in its inspired pages. In Jesus' Name I ask it. Amen.

THE COAL MINER AND THE PHD

For Reading and Meditation: Hebrews 4:1–13

"For the word of God is living and active.
Sharper than any double-edged sword ..." (v. 12)

Some of you reading these lines today may not have had the benefits of a good or extensive education. You may be deficient in your knowledge of many things – science, philosophy, the arts, etc. But here is the encouraging thing – none of these issues are important when it comes to the matter of defeating Satan.

THE TRIUMPH OF TRUTH

I remember being present some years ago in a church in South Wales when a debate was held between a university professor and an ordinary coal miner. The subject was: "Is the Bible true?" The university professor presented his arguments in a clear and cogent fashion and I remember feeling quite sorry for the miner as I envisaged some of the difficulties he might have when making his reply. After the professor had finished, the miner stood to his feet and for over an hour I witnessed one of the most amazing demonstrations of the Holy Spirit at work that I have ever seen in my life.

The miner began by asking everyone to bow their heads as he prayed a prayer which went something like this: "Lord, I have not had much education, but You know that I love Your Word and have spent my life searching its pages. Help me now to say something that will convince my friends here that Your Word is true." He then proceeded to demolish the arguments of the professor simply by quoting appropriate scriptures without making even a single comment. When he finished, there was thunderous applause. The professor's highly intellectual arguments had been torn to pieces by the sharp edges of the sword of the Spirit – by that, and by that alone.

When it comes to defeating Satan, education is unimportant.

O Father, the more I hear, the more I want to hear. For I was created by Your Word, designed according to Your Word, and I can never remain content until I am indwelt with Your Word. Teach me even more. In Jesus' Name. Amen.

GO STILL DEEPER
For Reading and Meditation: John 17:1–19

"... your word is truth." (v. 17)

Christians who do not accept the authority of the Scriptures undermine the very foundation they need to stand on when coming into conflict with the devil and all his forces. Without an authoritative Bible, we have no effective weapon with which to overcome Satan. It is as simple as that. If you are not certain that the Bible is the Word of God, if you do not believe that it is without error in all that it affirms, then you are like a soldier with a broken sword in his hand.

STEEPED IN SCRIPTURE

To use the sword of the Spirit effectively, we need to have as wide a knowledge of the Bible as possible. Let me take you back to Christ's encounter with Satan in the wilderness of temptation once again. When Satan advanced, Jesus took up the sword of the Spirit and knew exactly what scriptures to use. There were three different temptations and Jesus selected three different scriptures. He knew exactly the right word to select to rebut each temptation of the devil.

If we are to conquer Satan in the same way that Jesus conquered him, then we must know the Bible in its entirety. It is no good saying to the devil, "The verse I want to use against you is somewhere in the Bible." You must quote it to him and quote it precisely. Daily Bible reading notes will help you start the day, but you need a deeper and more intensive programme of study if you are to become proficient in the use of the Scriptures against Satan. Decide right now to commit yourself to exploring the Bible more deeply and thoroughly than you have ever done before.

To use the sword of the Spirit effectively, we need a wide knowledge of the Bible.

O Father, I see that the more I know of Your Word, the more effective I will be in resisting Satan. Show me how to go more deeply into the Scriptures than I have ever done before. In Jesus' Name I pray. Amen.

O ne might think that, having examined in detail the six pieces of the armour of God, this would be a natural place to end our discussion, but there is one more verse to consider: "Praying always with all prayer and supplication in the Spirit, being watchful to this end with all perseverance and supplication for all the saints" (Ephesians 6:18, NKJ).

EFFECTIVE WARFARE

What does Paul mean when he includes this further intriguing statement? He is saying (so I believe) that "praying in the Spirit" is something that ought to pervade all our spiritual warfare and is something we have to do and keep on doing if we are to win the battle against Satan and his forces. Paul is saying, "Put on the whole armour of God, every single piece, and in the proper order; but in addition to that, at all times and in all places, keep on praying."

The danger is that we can feel, once we have our spiritual armour on, that we are safe, we can relax, all is well, that the armour itself will protect us. But that is the height of folly and something Satan would love to get us to believe. And if we do believe it, then it means we are already defeated. The armour of God and its spiritual application must always be thought of in terms of our relationship and fellowship with God. If there is no communion with Him, then the six pieces of armour will be ineffective.

The armour of God is not something that is magical or mechanical; it functions as a spiritual defence only when worn with prayer.

The armour of God functions as a spiritual defence only when worn with prayer.

O Father, thank You for inspiring Your servant Paul to give us this insight, for we see that without it we would be defeated by the devil. Help me become a watchful and praying Christian. In Jesus' Name. Amen.

THE FOUR "ALLS"

For Reading and Meditation: Matthew 14:22–33

"… he went up on a mountainside by himself to pray …" (v. 23)

I

f, as we have seen, the effectiveness of our spiritual warfare depends not just on wearing the six pieces of armour, but also on constant believing prayer, then we must ask ourselves: What can we do to make our prayer lives more contributive?

PROWESS IN PRAYER

The place given to prayer in both the Old and New Testament is remarkable. All the great saints of the Old Testament knew how to pray – Abraham, David, Daniel, Jeremiah, Isaiah, to mention just a few. The same prowess in prayer can be seen also in the New Testament saints. But of course the greatest pray-er was none other than our Lord Jesus Christ. Although He possessed great knowledge and wisdom, He found it essential to turn aside time and time again to pray. On certain occasions He would spend whole nights in prayer or rise long before dawn in order to pray and maintain His communion with God. Is it surprising, therefore, that being so dependent on prayer, He should have told His disciples, "Men ought always to pray, and not to faint" (Luke 18:1, AV)? Praying is the only alternative to fainting – we must pray or else we faint.

Paul's teaching with regard to prayer in Ephesians 6:18 revolves around four "alls". We are to pray at *all* times, with *all* prayer, with *all* perseverance, and for *all* the saints. Most Christians, however, pray at some times, with some prayers, and some degree of perseverance for some of God's saints. When we replace "some" by "all" in these expressions, we are on our way to effective praying.

Pray at all times, with all prayer, with all perseverance, for all the saints.

My Father and my God, I see that through prayer, You offer me the most breathtaking power. Help me humbly to take it and use it wisely. In Jesus' Name I pray. Amen.

"PRAYER AND SUPPLICATION"
For Reading and Meditation: Colossians 4:1–12

"Devote yourselves to prayer, being watchful and thankful." (v. 2)

DAY 3 WEEK 7

Today we ask ourselves: what does it mean to "pray always with all prayer and supplication"? The phrase "praying always" presents no difficulty, for that, quite clearly, means praying as often as possible, regularly and constantly, but what does it mean to pray "with all prayer and supplication"? Paul means, I believe, that we should pray with all forms or kinds of prayer.

DIFFERENT FORMS OF PRAYER

You see, there are many different forms of prayer that are available to us. Firstly, there is verbal prayer when we present our prayers to God in carefully chosen words and phrases. Secondly, there is silent prayer, when no words cross our lips but prayer flows directly from our hearts. Thirdly, there is ejaculatory prayer, when we express sounds rather than words, as when we sigh or groan in prayer. Then there is public prayer, common prayer or "praying together" – or, as some prefer to call it, "praying in concert". So praying with all prayer means using every form of prayer available to us and praying in every way and manner that we can. We are to be at it always, and in endless ways.

But there is a certain form of prayer to which the apostle refers which deserves closer examination – the prayer of supplication. This refers to that aspect of prayer which we sometimes describe as "petition", when we pray with regard to special requests and needs. We must not overlook this, for it is so easy to be caught up in adoration and praise that we neglect to focus our prayers on the various needs that arise from time to time, not only in our own lives, but also in the lives of others.

We should pray constantly, with all forms of prayer.

Father, help me to see the senselessness of trying to muddle through life in my own strength when You have made Your power and resources available to me through prayer. Help me grow in prayer. In Jesus' Name. Amen.

"PRAYING IN THE SPIRIT"

For Reading and Meditation: Romans 8:18–30

"... we do not know what prayer to offer nor how to offer it worthily ... but the Spirit Himself ... pleads in our behalf ..." (v. 26, Amplified Bible)

Having looked yesterday at the phrase "praying always with all prayer and supplication", we turn now to focus on the words "in the Spirit". What does it mean to pray "in the Spirit"? Here again, there is a good deal of misunderstanding among Christians as to the true meaning of this phrase.

PROMPTED BY THE SPIRIT

Some claim the words "in the Spirit" mean praying with the emotions – or feeling greatly moved as one prays. There are times when one feels deeply affected emotionally as one prays, but this is not the meaning of the phrase "praying in the Spirit". The "Spirit" spoken of here is not the human spirit, but the Holy Spirit. Some believe that "praying in the Spirit" takes place when we pray in other tongues, and although it can include that, I believe it is much more than that.

Prayer that is "in the Spirit" is prayer that is prompted and guided by the Spirit. One commentator puts it in this way: "It means that the Holy Spirit directs the prayer, creates the prayer within us, and empowers us to offer it and to pray it." Some of the old Welsh preachers – Daniel Rowlands, Christmas Evans, and others – described it as "praying with unusual liberty and freedom".

Have you not experienced moments when, after struggling and halting in prayer, you were suddenly taken out of yourself and words just poured out of you? At that moment, you were "praying in the Spirit".

Praying in the Spirit is "praying with unusual liberty and freedom".

Dear Father, I have so much to learn about prayer that unless You take my hand and guide me, I can soon lose my way. Teach me how to enter the deeper levels of prayer. In Jesus' Name. Amen.

NOT SOME ... BUT ALL

For Reading and Meditation: Ephesians 4:17–32

"... for we are members of one another."
(v. 25, NKJ)

We have two more phrases to consider before we bring to a close our study of Ephesians 6:10–20: (1) "Keep alert with all perseverance" and (2) "making supplication for all the saints" (Ephesians 6:18, RSV).

SPIRITUAL WATCHFULNESS

The first phrase draws our attention to the fact that we should never allow ourselves to become indolent and lethargic in relation to the matter of prayer, but always eager and ready to make our requests and petitions known to Him. But what is the purpose of this spiritual alertness and watchfulness? This question brings us to the second phrase: "Making supplication for all the saints". Our watchfulness and concern must not be only on our own behalf, but on behalf of all other Christians also.

A COMMON ENEMY

Why does Paul exhort us to pray for *all* rather than some Christians – those, for example, whom we know are enduring a particular attack of Satan? The answer is because all Christians need praying for. Every believer is under attack; no one is exempted. The letter of Jude tells us that we are partakers of a "common salvation" (v. 3, AV). But not only do we enjoy a common salvation: we are fighting a common enemy, and in our encounter with this common enemy we experience common difficulties – hence the need to be intensely aware of each other's needs. We cannot, of course, take the armour of God and put it on another Christian, but we can pray for one another and thus call in spiritual reinforcements. We can pray that their eyes might be opened to the danger they are in and that they might be able to equip themselves to stand against Satan and his powerful forces.

By praying we can call in spiritual reinforcements to fight the common enemy.

O Father, forgive me, I pray, that sometimes I am so taken up with my own spiritual struggles that I forget my brothers and sisters face the same difficulties also. Save me from my self-centredness, dear Lord. In Jesus' Name I pray. Amen.

PRAY FOR ME THAT ...

For Reading and Meditation: Romans 12:1–13

"Then you will be able to test and approve what God's will is – his good, pleasing and perfect will." (v. 2)

The apostle ends his section on spiritual warfare (Ephesians 6:10–20) on the following personal note: "Pray on my behalf, that utterance may be given to me in the opening of my mouth, to make known with boldness the mystery of the gospel ... that in proclaiming it I may speak boldly, as I ought to speak" (vv. 19–20, NASB).

IN NEED OF STRENGTH

Paul was wise enough to know his own need of supernatural strength if he was to stand against the enemy, and was humble enough to ask his brothers and sisters to pray for him in this matter. Imagine this great apostle, probably the most powerful and effective disciple of Christ the world has ever seen, asking his friends to pray for him. And why not? The greater a Christian is, the more he realises his dependence on the prayers of others. Paul knew full well the power that was against him and he does not hesitate to ask for the prayers of the church in Ephesus.

SPECIFIC SUPPLICATION

Notice that his request for prayer is clear and specific – "that utterance may be given to me in the opening of my mouth, to make known with boldness the mystery of the gospel". Whenever you ask someone to pray for you, be equally specific. Don't just say, "Pray for me", but "Pray for me that ..." Note, too, that Paul's request was not that he might be delivered from prison, but that through his testimony in prison the Gospel of Christ might be advanced. He knew that the most important thing at the moment was not to triumph over prison but to triumph in it. He knew he was where God wanted him for that time, and he would allow no self-interest to interfere with the divine schedule.

The greater a Christian is, the more he realises his dependence on the prayers of others.

O Father, teach me, as You taught Your servant Paul, to know Your will and purposes so clearly that I might know just how and what to pray for. I ask this in and through the strong and mighty Name of Jesus. Amen.

THE FINAL WORD

For Reading and Meditation: Ephesians 3:8–21

"To the intent that now the manifold wisdom of God might be made known by the church to the principalities and powers …" (v. 10, NKJ)

O n this, our last day together, we gather up what we have been saying on this important theme of "The Armour of God". Once we become Christians, we said, we are involved in a fight – a fight against Satan and his forces. God, however, has given us a defence against Satan and his wiles, which consists of six separate pieces of spiritual equipment.

THE COMPLETE DEFENCE SYSTEM

Firstly, He has given us the belt of truth – a willingness to let God's truth govern and regulate every part of our lives. Secondly, the breastplate of righteousness – seeing clearly that we are not saved by our own righteousness but Christ's. Thirdly, we must have our feet shod with the preparation of the gospel of peace – our determination to stand firmly in the faith.

Fourthly, we must raise the shield of faith – the quick action by which we act upon God's truth and refuse Satan's lies. Fifthly, we must put on the helmet of salvation – the glorious hope that, one day, God will right all wrongs and establish His eternal kingdom. And sixthly, we must take up the sword of the Spirit, the Word of God, and wield the written Scriptures in the same way that our Lord did in His wilderness temptations.

Yet we noted also that having done all this, it is still possible that we could be defeated by the devil unless we know how to pray in the power of the Spirit. And we must pray, not just now and again, not simply when we are in trouble, not only when things go wrong, but continuously, fervently, powerfully and perseveringly. Our prayers must catch alight and burst into flame. Against such prayers, the principalities and powers are helpless.

To be a Christian is to be involved in a fight.

My Father, now that I have seen the resources that are available to me in Christ, I realise that my responsibility to avail myself of those resources is greater than ever. Help me to put everything I have learned into action. For Your own dear Name's sake. Amen.